Vroom!
HOT CARS

CHEVY
CORVETTE

CHARLES PIDDOCK

Guided Reading Level: V

rourkeeducationalmedia.com

Scan for Related Titles and
Teacher Resources

TABLE OF CONTENTS

ROCK N' ROLL AND A BLUE CORVETTE

Put the pedal to the metal with the top down dreaming Hands on the wheel with the engine screaming ...Don't let life pass you by like a blue Corvette, like a blue Corvette.

—from "Blue Corvette" by Adam Gregory

They don't write rock songs about sub-compact cars or plug-in electric cars, but they certainly do about the Chevy Corvette. Besides "Blue Corvette," there have been more than 50 rock songs praising the vehicle. The Corvette is much more than just a sports car.

It symbolizes a way of life and an attitude that values freedom and independence. When you travel in a Corvette you become part of an American legend. Once behind the wheel, you might even feel inspired to write a song—or sing one.

2016 Chevy Corvette

Fans usually refer to a Corvette by its nickname of "Vette."

LIKE A COKE BOTTLE

The first thing most people notice about the Corvette is its looks. It has been described as a rolling work of art. Low, sleek, and powerful looking, the Corvette is deliberately styled and shaped like another symbol of America—a classic Coke bottle.

Like the Coke bottle, the Corvette has a full chest, a narrow waist, and an expanded rear. Its expanded rear gives the car an illusion of power, while its front expands, then tapers to a point. Its tapered front makes it **aerodynamic**, reducing **drag** and allowing the Corvette to cut through the air with ease.

The Coke bottle design was first used in jet planes to make them more aerodynamic.

The Corvette design has changed over the years, but it always kept its hourglass shape. It has a full front and expanded rear.

BEAUTY AND BRAWN

It is said that beauty is only skin deep. Not so with the Corvette. To car people, it's as beautiful under the hood and inside the cabin as it is on the outside. Under the hood of a Corvette Stingray is an engine that puts out 455-**horsepower** and 460 pound-feet of torque.

Torque is a measure of the turning force on car wheels. The higher the torque produced by the engine, the quicker a car can **accelerate**. For the Corvette Stingray, it means the car can go from zero to 60 miles (96.56 kilometers) per hour in just 3.7 seconds!

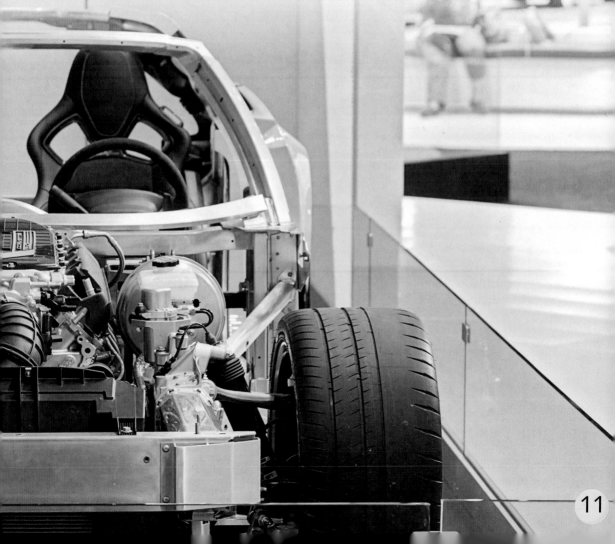

The sleek beauty of the Corvette has been compared to a powerfully muscled leopard.

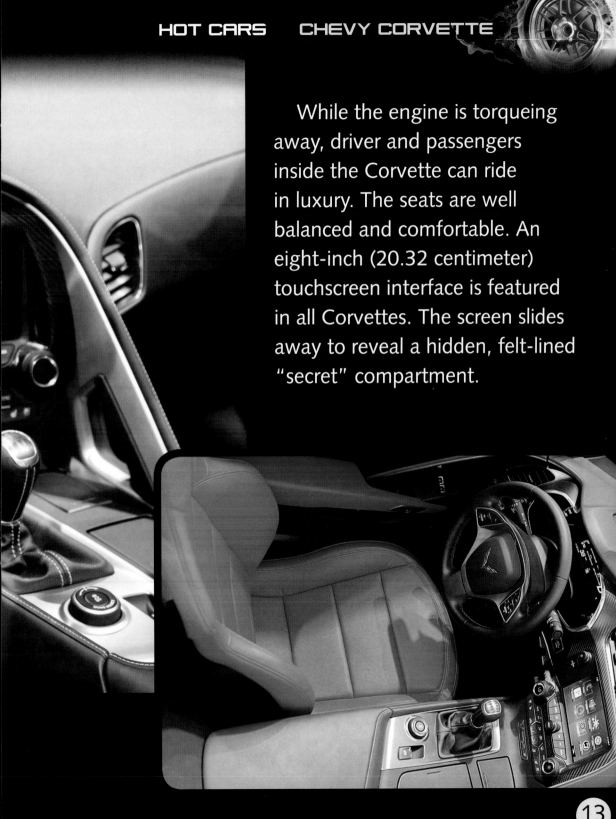

While the engine is torqueing away, driver and passengers inside the Corvette can ride in luxury. The seats are well balanced and comfortable. An eight-inch (20.32 centimeter) touchscreen interface is featured in all Corvettes. The screen slides away to reveal a hidden, felt-lined "secret" compartment.

THE BIRTH OF A NEW CAR

The Corvette and rock n' roll were born around the same time. Bill Haley and the Comets formed the first rock n' roll band in 1952. In 1951, an auto designer named Harley J. Earl began plans for a low-cost American sports car that would satisfy American consumers' desire for a car that would be more than just transportation. Earl worked for General Motors, parent company of Chevrolet. He wanted GM to build a low-cost American sports car that could compete with Europe's MGs, Jaguars and Ferraris.

1953 Chevrolet C1 Corvette Roadster

The entire 1953 production took place in the back of a Flint customer delivery garage.
Of the first 300 Corvettes, approximately 225 are known to still exist today!

On June 28, 1953, workers in Flint, Michigan, assembled the first Corvette based on Earl's design. The first completed production car rolled off the assembly line two days later, one of just 300 Corvettes made that year. It was hand-assembled and featured a white exterior and red interior, automatic transmission, and a windshield that wrapped around the car instead of side windows. In 1954, the Corvette went into mass production at a Chevy plant in St. Louis, Missouri.

Blue Flame in-line 6 engine on a 1953 Corvette convertible

The man who named the new car a Corvette was Myron Scott, a photographer in the Chevrolet Public Relations Department. He named it after a fast-moving naval ship called a corvette.

THROUGH THE GENERATIONS

The Corvette has been through seven generations since 1953. A generation marks a significant change in style or engineering. The Corvette is now in its seventh generation, which began in 2014.

First Generation (1953 - 1962)

The first generation of Corvette marked a time when Chevy was gradually improving the Corvette from the first model—adding a more efficient and powerful engine, power windows, and other improvements.

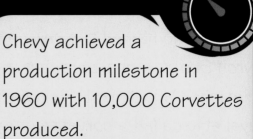

Chevy achieved a production milestone in 1960 with 10,000 Corvettes produced.

The 1960 Corvette was the first Corvette to reach over 10,000 sales.

Second Generation (1963 - 1967)

Chevy designed the second generation Corvette to be the coolest-looking yet and introduced a new name: Stingray. The Stingray had, among other changes, hidden headlights and four-wheel disk brakes.

Corvettes have always been a favorite of athletes, astronauts, and celebrities. For many years, it was the prize for the most valuable player in the World Series and was the unofficial car of the Mercury, Gemini, and Apollo astronauts in the 1960s.

42543·H
NSW · HISTORIC VEHICLE

The big news for the 1965 Vette was the addition of standard 4-wheel disc brakes and a 425-horsepower V-8.

The 1965 Corvette had disk brakes on all four wheels, not just two wheels as was common in cars then. It also introduced a much more powerful engine.

19

The 1978 Corvette celebrated its 25th anniversary with a completely redesigned body that included new "fastback" styling.

Third Generation (1968—1982)

Look out on the road! The third generation Corvette was the sleekest yet and looked like it might just take off like a plane or a rocket. The 1978 Corvette also marked the car's 25th anniversary. All 1978s featured a special **commemorative** badge on the front nose.

1990 Corvette

The fourth generation was delayed for a year, so no Corvettes were built in 1983.

Fourth Generation (1984—1996)

The fourth generation Corvette marked the first complete redesign of the car since 1963. The car was now sleeker and smoother looking with a more powerful engine. In 1992, Chevy introduced an even

Supplemental Restraint Systems (better known as airbags) were the law of the land for all cars manufactured after September 1989, and they were added to the Corvette on the driver's side for the 1990 model year.

Fifth Generation (1997—2004)

The fifth generation Corvette was no friend of speed limits. Its aerodynamic shape and powerful engine gave it a top speed of 181 miles (291 kilometers) per hour!

In 1999, Corvette offered buyers a **hardtop** for the first time.

The 1999 Corvette featured a "Heads Up Display." The system displayed speedometer, tachometer, (with shift light), water temperature, oil pressure, fuel level and turn signal on the windshield in front of the driver.

Sixth Generation (2005—2013)

The sixth generation allowed buyers of several Corvette models the opportunity to assist in the building of their car's engine.

A style change beginning in 2005 for Corvette was to have fixed headlamps instead of retractable headlamps.

Buyers paid extra to help assembly line workers build the car's engine, then took delivery of the car at the National Corvette Museum in Bowling Green, Kentucky.

The 2015 Corvette had a 505-horsepower engine, the most powerful engine ever in a Corvette convertible.

Z06 keeps drivers connected using a retractable 8-inch (20.32 centimeter) high-definition color touchscreen. Drivers can talk, text, and stream music without taking their hands off the wheel.

Seventh Generation (2014–present)

Current Corvette models carry on the true American Corvette sports car tradition that began in 1953 well into the 21st century.

The National Corvette Museum in Bowling Green, Kentucky, is near the Corvette assembly plant. It draws thousands of visitors every year from all parts of the globe.

ON HOLLYWOOD BOULEVARD

The Corvette has a central place in American pop culture. It has been prominently featured in many Hollywood films such as *Terms of Endearment, Animal House, American Graffiti, Apollo 13*, and *Corvette Summer*. But the Corvette really starred in a television series called *Route 66*, which ran from 1960 to 1964 on CBS. It featured a college grad who inherited a Corvette convertible and traveled the country on Interstate Route 66. Each year, Chevrolet gave the show a brand-new Corvette to use.

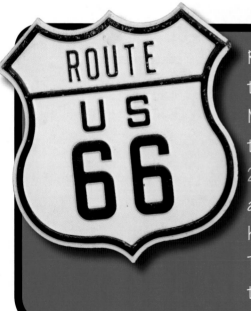

Route 66 was once known as the "Main Street of America" and "the Mother Road." It ran from Chicago to Santa Monica, California, covering 2,448 miles (3,939.68 kilometers). In addition to the TV show, it inspired a hit song, "Get Your Kicks on Route 66." The famous highway was removed from the U.S. Highway System in 1985.

AN E-RAY?

The Corvette has a storied past. But will it have a storied future? Chevy designers and engineers are betting on it. A mid-engine Corvette called the Zora is slated for introduction in 2017. In automobile design, an M4, or mid-engine, is a design that places the engine in the middle of the car, not in the front or rear, as in most cars. Mid-engine gives the car more instant power and **traction**. Zora, however, may only be the start. Reportedly, General Motors is secretly working on the E-Ray, an all-electric or **hybrid** version of the Corvette.

Route 66

GLOSSARY

accelerate (ak-SEL-uh-rayt): to begin to move more quickly

aerodynamic (air-oh-dye-NAM-ik): designed to move through the air very easily and quickly

commemorative (kuh-mem-or-uh-tiv): marking the memory of a person or event

drag (drag): the force exerted by air on a moving object

hardtop (HAHRD-tahp): a car with a rigid roof that is detachable

horsepower (HORS-pou-ur): a unit of power equal to 550 foot-pounds per second

hybrid (HYE-brid): something that is made by combining two or more things; hybrid cars use both gasoline and electricity

traction (TRAK-shun): the grip of a tire on a road

INDEX

SHOW WHAT YOU KNOW

1. What well-known object is a model for the shape of a Corvette?
2. What is torque a measure of?
3. Harley J. Earl was an automobile designer for what company?
4. How long does it take for the Corvette Stingray to go from 0 to 60?
5. What highway was once called the "Main Street of America"?

WEBSITES TO VISIT

www.corvettemuseum.org

www.chevrolet.com/corvette-stingray.html

www.history.com/this-day-in-history/workers-assemble-first-corvette-in-flint-michigan/print

ABOUT THE AUTHOR

Charles Piddock is the former Editor-in-Chief of Weekly Reader Corporation. He has written many books for both young people and adults. He and his wife live by a lake in south-central Maine.

Meet The Author!
www.meetREMauthors.com

© 2017 Rourke Educational Media

www.rourkeeducationalmedia.com

PHOTO CREDITS: Cover: Arpad Benedek; Header art © Petrosg; speedometer art © didis; pages 2-3 © Speedphi; pages 4-5 © Darren Brode, pages 6-7 Corvette © Barry Blackburn, coke bottle © M. Unal Ozmen; pages 8-9 © Boykov; pages 10-11 © Darren Brode; pages 12-13 steering wheel shot © Jia Li, leather interior © Darren Brode; pages 14-15 white 1953 Vette © Sicnag, engine shot © Kowloonese; pages 16-17 © 1960 Vette front shot © Mauvries, interior shot © JOSEPH S.L. TAN MATT, logo © Eckhard Henkel / Wikimedia Commons / CC BY-SA 3.0 DE, shot of rear © Kevin M. McCarthy; pages 18-19 © sv1ambo, logo © Atomazul; page 20- © Greg Gjerdingen, page 21 © Steven N. Severinghaus https://commons.wikimedia.org/wiki/File:Corvette_ZR1.jpg; page 22-23 red 1999 Corvette © Sicnag; pages24-25 © Thesupermat; page 26 © © Redwood8 | Dreamstime.com; page 27 © M 93; page 28 © kojihirano, page 29 © Fredddie http://creativecommons.org/licenses/by-sa/3.0/ Images on following pages from Shutterstock.com: pages 4-13, 16, 17, emblem on page 18

Edited by: Keli Sipperley

Cover design by: Rhea Magaro
Interior design by: Nicola Stratford   www.nicolastratford.com

Library of Congress PCN Data

Chevy Corvette / Charles Piddock
(VROOM! Hot Cars)
ISBN 978-1-68191-745-0 (hard cover)
ISBN 978-1-68191-846-4 (soft cover)
ISBN 978-1-68191-937-9 (e-Book)
Library of Congress Control Number: 2016932708

Rourke Educational Media
Printed in the United States of America, North Mankato, Minnesota

Also Available as:

ROURKE'S
e-Books